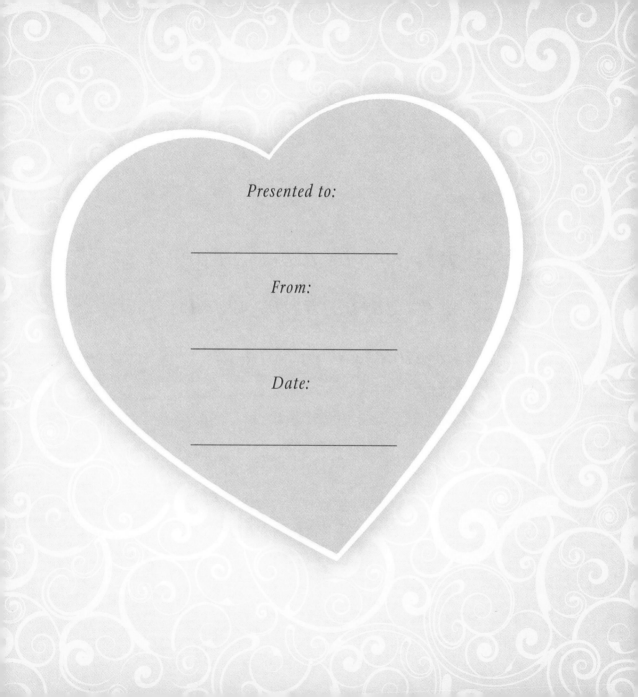

Presented to:

_____

From:

_____

Date:

_____

Worry weighs a person down;
an encouraging word
cheers a person up.

PROVERBS 12:25 NLT

kisses
of
Encouragement

Heartwarming Messages
That Encourage & Inspire

HOWARD BOOKS
A DIVISION OF SIMON & SCHUSTER
New York   London   Toronto   Sydney

Our purpose at Howard Books is to:
- *Increase faith* in the hearts of growing Christians
- *Inspire holiness* in the lives of believers
- *Instill hope* in the hearts of struggling people everywhere
  Because He's coming again!

HOWARD

Published by Howard Books, a division of Simon & Schuster, Inc.
1230 Avenue of the Americas, New York, NY 10020
www.howardpublishing.com

Kisses of Encouragement © 2007 by Dave Bordon & Associates, LLC

ISBN-13: 978-1-4165-5865-1
ISBN-10: 1-4165-5865-9

10 9 8 7 6 5 4 3 2

HOWARD and colophon are registered trademarks of Simon & Schuster, Inc.

Manufactured in the United States of America

For information regarding special discounts for bulk purchases, please contact: Simon & Schuster Special Sales at 1-800-456-6798 or business@simonandschuster.com.

Project developed by Bordon Books, Tulsa, Oklahoma
Project writing and compilation by Christy Phillippe in association with Bordon Books
Edited by Chrys Howard
Cover design by Greg Jackson, Thinkpen Design

INTRODUCTION

A kiss. It's short. Sweet. And from the heart. That's what *Kisses of Encouragement* is all about. Each page of this book is a message of hope to brighten your day and let you know how much I care. As you read, I hope you'll remember all of the amazing gifts and talents that you have, and that you'll realize what a very special person you are to me!

May our Lord Jesus Christ himself and God our Father, who loved us and by his grace gave us eternal encouragement and good hope, encourage your hearts . . .

2 THESSALONIANS 2:16-17 NIV

No matter what
comes your way today,

whether happy . . .

or sad,

whether big . . .

or small,

whether soft and fuzzy . . .

or hard and prickly,

remember that God is by
your side—

and I am, too!

I'm here when you need me—

with a helping hand . . .

a listening ear . . .

a shoulder to lean on . . .

and the reminder that if life
throws you a curveball,

you can still hit a
home run—

and I am cheering you on!

You are an **amazing** human being—
so loving and caring,

talented in so many ways,

with an indomitable spirit,

a laugh-out-loud
sense of humor,

and an incomparable
zest for life.

You're one of a kind!

Through faith in God
and yourself,

a winning attitude,

a lot of perseverance,

**and a little help from
your friends,**

you can make it

through anything.

You can climb the highest
mountain . . .

solve the hardest puzzle . . .

conquer your fears . . .

even reach the stars

if you never stop learning . . .

if you stick your neck out . . .

and you take a chance on love . . .

and if you give it your all!

You have something beautiful
to offer—

something unique . . .

something dazzling . . .

something needed—

something only you can create.

You may have to color outside the lines once in a while

before your masterpiece is complete.

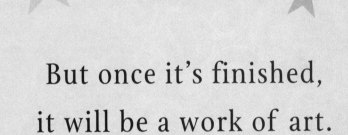

But once it's finished,
it will be a work of art.

Even when changes come,

when storm clouds threaten,

or when things don't go as planned,

remember, something new
may be just ahead,

and unexpected beginnings can be
the start of something grand.

Good things are coming
your way

because God has a wonderful
plan for your life

and a purpose for every
challenge you face.

So don't give up . . .

believe in the One who knows you

best and loves you most . . .

and dare to live life to the fullest!

The world needs you—

your hopes,